HEROISM,
HUMILITY,
AND HONOR

Learn2Succeed Publishing, LLC

Cover Design and Interior Formatting: Kevin Anderson & Associates
and Elise Grinstead

Cover Image: Shutterstock

Editor: Tiffany Morgan

The Star Spangled Banner, National Anthem of the United States: Public Domain

ISBN: 978-0-9974330-0-5

HEROISM, HUMILITY, AND HONOR

Poems to Thank You

T.E. BROOKS

IN LOVING MEMORY

In Memory of My Dad, Gene
(He was a United States Air Force Veteran)
My First Elegy as a Teenager
Unpublished Work ~ Happiness Is… Reading My Book of Poems!

THE GREAT HERO (MY DAD)

There was this man whose name was Gene
Who was the quietest man you ever have seen,
When he was at home he would sit in his chair,
You could always look and find him there.

He used to go to Inland and work hard,
But when he came home he would work in the yard,
He would wash his car and keep it clean,
And mow the lawn to keep it green.

Until that day as he lay on his sick bed,
"I'll be alright," is all that he said,
When he took his very last breath,
From the beginning to end, he faced his own death.

As he lay in the baby blue casket,
I looked at the many pretty flowers in the basket,
But at least he does not have to suffer anymore,
Because he will always be known as my great hero!

IN LOVING MEMORY

In memory of my mom, Ann, who inspired me to write poetry.
She was an extraordinary, courageous mom and military spouse.
Unpublished Work ~ Happiness Is… Reading My Book of Poems!

MY MOTHER'S WORDS

As long as I can remember,
From the age of four or five,
My mother often telling me,
To always be helpful and kind,
No matter what people say or do,
You should always be polite, kind, and true.

As I continue to grow older,
Things always seem to be,
Just the opposite of what mother has taught me,
Oh, how can this be?

You must remember child,
Our Heavenly Father above,
Who guides us with his finger,
And caresses with His love,
He never will forsake you or leave you alone,
That is why you must make,
Your heart, Christ's home.

DEDICATION

My Darling O, "Thank you for your love and service"
I love you,
"T"

O'S FANTABULOUS JOURNEY

Philippians 4:13 says, "I can do ALL things through CHRIST which strengtheneth me."

From Dayton, OH to Cincinnati to Lackland, AFB
Keesler in Mississippi too,
To say the least
The journey of a lifetime about to begin

Well O thought it was onto Germany
No, my son, it's onto Crete
That little island in Greece
Where Paul went as a missionary, to plant his feet
The place where I will mold and shape you
Into the husband to be
Just for that sweet and quiet young lady named T
She loves me, She loves me not, She loves me
Because we're going all the way to Minot
Where is that?
O, we must get a map
The Air Force has set us up
For the biggest and coldest 87° below winter trap!

Well, we survive for five

And now we must go to the Nation's Capital

Washington, DC to Headquarters

WOW!

The Pentagon

The Department of Defense for the Nation

Congratulations, what a sensation

To become a part of the elite

Destined for greatness and a mission to complete

However, that dreadful 9-11 day

We praise the LORD for you being at home, not at work yet

Remembering, the fallen and their sacrifice

The mission is still at hand

The LORD is not through with you yet

Now my son O

I am going to send you remote

"Where HE leads me I will follow"

Even to the distant land of Korea

Oh no! A year you say to trust and obey and to be

Happy in JESUS?
I want to come home to be back with my family

Well, DTSA is the place that you go
And the last stop of this fantabulous journey
O's journey ends with the United States Air Force
Now a veteran of military service

"O'S FLAG OF SERVICE"

TABLE OF CONTENTS

A SOLDIER'S HEROIC HEART

Love, honor, and duty
Tender qualities
Near and dear
To the heart of a soldier

Oftentimes,
During life-threatening combat,
A soldier chooses to stay
To care for another wounded comrade
To value others' needs before their very own

For at the end of a long day's work,
Especially, on the battlefield,
The soldier understands
How to carry out
The call of duty and the mission,
A soldier's heart remains
Dedicated to the cause

Humility must come before honor
Tenderly put, each and every one of their
Self-sacrificing actions,
Shines forth the love deep inside your heart
- love of family
- love of country
- love of mankind
- love of self

The heart of a soldier is
Undeniably, incredibly, courageously brave
The soldier's self-less sacrifice
Paid such a high price
Worthy of the "Purple Heart"
Soldier, wear it proudly
Covering your heroic, humble heart

THE SOLDIER'S UNIFORM

The soldier stands tall,
Wearing the uniform with pride,
Answering the call to duty,
With absolutely nothing to hide,
At times, not always a luxury

While thinking about the real cause,
The soldier reflects,
Without hesitation, or even one pause,
Ready to protect and defend,
Old glory – our flag,
Our red, white, and blue friend

Ready for action,
Extending a most- needed hand,
The soldier remains
Prepared and ready to take a stand,
Left, left, left, right, left,
Left, left, left, right, left.

The soldier marches to the beat,
Sometimes in the frigid cold,
Even in the sweltering heat

Standing tall,
Standing proud,
Giving your all,
Well proportioned,
Highly decorated,
With much success,
Pressed and crisp
For freedom
The soldier's uniform

COMMITMENT TO SERVE

What does it mean to serve?
To serve means,
To give of one's self, for the good of others
Never expecting anything in return
Thinking of others,
Before you think about yourself

Often realizing that many times,
A soldier's actions seem to go unnoticed
Yet, through it all, one mission at a time,
A soldier's brave and compassionate sacrifice
Exemplifies the true cost of freedom,
The commitment to serve

The true servant's attitude
Patriotic commitment displayed
Exemplifies the soldier's characteristics
Love of country, your fellow man, and yourself,
Motivated to stay committed to the oath,
"You will protect, support, and defend from
all enemies foreign and domestic, so help you God."

Remembering, Christ came to serve,
Not to be served, and through serving,
He gave His life so that all could have
Life more abundantly

With your dedication,
Determination, and devotion,
Likewise, you give your life unselfishly
Paving the way, both near and far
Allowing others to experience
The true essence of freedom
The commitment to serve

A TRUE PATRIOT

When a soldier demonstrates
An allegiance to the flag
By showing a
Love of one's country
Like no other,
Steadfastly, defending freedom
The soldier is a true patriot

A soldier's steadfast,
Unwavering devotion
To fight, protect, and defend
Exhibiting a tremendous sacrifice
In order to protect freedom
Going above and beyond
The call of duty,
The soldier is a true patriot

Forever faithful to the cause
A soldier wears
The uniform with pride

Proud to protect, honor,
Defend freedom,
No matter the cost,
The soldier is a true patriot

A soldier represents
Freedom on both sides,
The inside and the outside
The soldier exemplifies
The courage and
Commitment to serve
Deep within revealing
The heart of a soldier,
The soldier is a true patriot.

MIGHTY SOLDIER OF VALOR

Mighty soldier of valor
Preparing for the battlefield,
Not uncommon for you to be
Wearing your heart on your sleeve

Combat is calling for you to yield
Now you must prepare to go
The time has come,
It is time for you to leave

Courageously, you are
Holding back your cries
Trying to head out the door
While saying your final goodbyes

Duffel bag in your right hand
Boarding the military aircraft
Saluting your loved ones,
Bound for battle in a
Foreign land

Mighty soldier of valor
On the battlefield,
Off to a blazing start
On your first night in battle
You receive your orders
Your commander says,
"Soldier, defeat the enemy!"

Immediately, sirens sound
Weapons fire ruefully
While laying low on the ground
No silence in sight,
Your target is in view
A suicide bomber
Ready to ambush, more
Innocent lives tonight

Mighty soldier of valor
On the battlefield,
Your finger trembling, but steady
On the trigger of your weapon
You aim, quickly, you fire
The enemy falls to the ground
Victory!

Mighty soldier of valor
On the battlefield,
Overcoming fear quickly,
Now on the lookout for
Any bobbed wire
Without experiencing
Anything such as this before,
The torment and devastation of war
Is over somehow, really?
It is over for now

Mighty soldier of valor
On the battlefield,
Time to board the aircraft
Trying desperately,
To not look back
For now, anyway
It is time, for you, soldier
To return back to
The place that you call home

HERO, INCREDIBLE YOU

Sometimes, life throws
The toughest blows
For you to handle
Yet, through all the strife
You find the strength to overcome
Each day, somehow,
Remembering that your life
Shines brightly as the stars above
But, off to war you must go
Hero, incredible you

You have taken a stand
Without a chance of ever
Giving up hope
By deciding to raise your right hand,
Accounting for each and every
Trial and circumstance
Never wavering, but persevering
By learning how to cope
In spite of the unknown awaiting

You are a soldier now
Hero, incredible you

You have taken on life
With each new day
Counting it a true blessing
Leading by example
As you pass on the torch to the
Next generation that will follow after you
No matter what, "Come on life, come what may."
You are a survivor of the bloody battlefield
Soldier, you are here to stay
How disheartening,
Every aspect of war seems!
Hero, incredible you

WOUNDED WARRIOR

Service connected injury
Service connected illness
The life of a soldier
Changed forever

Left home
Whole and complete
Returned home
With a new battle to face

Amputations
Mental health conditions
Spinal cord injuries
Traumatic brain injuries

Thank you
Just doesn't seem
To suffice
For your heroic sacrifice

Soldier, you are not alone
We support you
We love you
We are here to help you

On your road to recovery,
We empower you
We will help you to succeed
By honoring you in
Your time of need

Accept the Wounded Warrior
Earned Purple Heart
For your bravery and heroism
We honor and appreciate you

Your duty
Your courage
Your commitment
Your service
Will not ever be in vain

Valuing your
Full potential
Being more than average,
Being more than ordinary,
You have the hand-prints
Of freedom all over you
Including the extraordinary
Even, all the pain, too,
Standing on the front lines
Sacrificing your life and limbs
For freedom
Wounded, but not forgotten.

COMING HOME

After surviving a
Suicide bomb, grenade attack,
A severe bullet wound,
There is comfort in knowing
The soldier will be free
To return home

Although the intensity of war
Has been a constant reminder
Of life on the battlefield,
The soldier is learning to cope
While facing life with exuberant hope

The constant uncertainty
Of not knowing
What life will be like after the
Fighting stops,
Piece by piece, wound by wound
The healing begins

For some, marriages are still in tact
Families hanging on by a thread
Knowing that it will take some time
To resume life,
As the soldier once knew it to be

However, a sigh of relief
Coming home is a reality
Savor this precious moment
Only time will heal the
Unforgettable wounds of war

HERO, WELCOME HOME

You left unscathed and unharmed
However, you returned a bit shaken,
Battered, wounded, but heroic
You had to live your life in constant
Fear of when or where the
Enemy might appear out of nowhere,
In an instant, to hurt, and kill
You and your comrades

Dreams about the war zone haunt you
Sometimes insomnia sends reminders
About the blood shed on the battlefield
Regardless of the effects of war,
Freedom is all that matters to you
Freedom is worth going to war for
Freedom is worth every bit of sacrifice,
Remembering the hours of excruciating pain
The soldier proclaims, "I am a soldier!"

Thank you for each opportunity
That you give your life
Choosing to serve your country

Thank you for teaching others
To appreciate freedom
Rather than to take freedom for granted
Thank you is only a small token of appreciation
Coming from the heart
Thank you soldier
For all that you have done, and
Continue to do, for all humanity
Hero, welcome home!

PEACE: THE MISSION

Peace
No more war fighting
Happening on the battlefield
Peace
No more casualties
Peace
No more war uncertainty
Peace
No more sleepless nights
Peace
No more war on terrorism
Peace
No more troubled hearts
Peace
No more fear of the enemy

Peace is:
Public security
Enduring freedom
Absence of conflict
Calm before the storm
End to war

The soldiers of peace
Marching in cadence
Tranquility at rest
Calmness
War, no longer an option
Mission complete
No more conflict
Peace, the power of freedom.

THE SPECIAL OPERATIONS SOLDIER

Demands of your calling,
Special Operations
Highly skilled, versatile, and complex
While facing some impossible,
Insurmountable odds
Whether at sea, in the air,
Or on the ground,
Soldier, you are in high demand,
Called upon often
To utilize your remarkable skills
In order to capture
A malicious, ruthless enemy
In an instant, without much notice
It really doesn't matter
Whether it is in the dark
Or completely by surprise
Prepared to complete the mission

Who are you?

Your identity,

Despite being, completely unknown

To the world,

Still the soldier fulfills the duty

Defeating the enemy

The Special Operations soldier

Supports missions

Beyond ordinary control

Difficult indeed,

Fighting, protecting, defending freedom

Capturing a malicious enemy

Heroically,

In service, humility, and honor

A UNITED STATES MARINE

You are a
United States Marine
There are not enough words
To describe
Your fearlessness
Thank you for your courage

As you lead the way to overcome the
Terrorism in the world
The way that you display heroism
Should never go overlooked

No matter what,
You keep the heart that overflows with
Freedom, pride, dignity, valor, and love
And yes, you represent
The few and the proud,
You are a Unites States Marine.
You lead by example
You go, serve, and defend

Yes, we can depend on you to
Protect, fight, and march into battle

No matter the cost
By air, on land, or even across the seas
Liberty, sweet liberty, helps you to
Face the ultimate challenge
Essential to our freedom
And march onto victory
Yes, you are a United States Marine
Your duty is earned and never given.

UNITED WE STAND

United we stand
Soldiers comprehend
Divided we will fall
Let us not forget
One nation, with liberty,
Freedom and justice for all

A land of diversity
No longer a nation
Of only black or white
Now, all inclusive
A soldier paves
The way for freedom
Now within our sight
America, of yesterday
The history of the past,
Let us strive to embrace peace
Accepting our differences
While embracing hand in hand
The common goal of unity,
Expecting freedom to last
United we stand

In the end
A soldier's journey
Celebrates our differences
Celebrates freedom
Believes in one another
Ultimately, holds the key to unity
Because togetherness,
Epitomizes, united we stand

AMERICA, THE LAND I LOVE

My country, 'tis of thee
Sweet land of liberty
America, the land that I love

No matter your nation, color, or creed
This is the land of opportunity
Liberty, freedom, and equality
There is justice for all

America, America, America
The land that I love

My country, 'tis of thee
Sweet land of liberty
America, the land that I love

No matter whether rich or poor
You don't have to worry anymore
The American Dream
Can be forevermore
Let freedom ring

America, America, America
The land that I love

AMERICA: FACTS OF FREEDOM

Amendments, the Bill of Rights, civil rights,
Freedom of the land
In God We Trust, the motto of the land
Words, sounds, letters spoken aloud
In the national language, called English

The rose and none appose,
Red flower of freedom,
Independence was declared
Way back on July 4, 1776,
America, free indeed, to govern her people
The laws of the land
Signed on September 17, 1787,
The place, Philadelphia, PA

Freedom and justice for all,
Slavery a thing of the past
The Emancipation Proclamation
Signed on January 1, 1863,

Put an end to slavery
These are but a few
Facts of freedom
In the country known for bravery

America, a country
For democracy and liberty
The people in society have a voice
There are civil rights and freedoms
For her citizens
Equality of opportunity
Helping all who live here
Experience success
Freedom, a right, and a privilege

HEROISM, HUMILITY, AND HONOR

Heroism
Dauntlessness, fearlessness
Valor and fortitude
Tenacity, perseverance

Humility
Humbleness in spirit
Submissiveness
Obeying those in authority
Meek, not looking to be the
Center of attention

Honor
Credit for your service
Celebrating the hero inside and out
Realizing that freedom costs
Such a high price,
On a mission
Fighting and defending
The precious privilege of freedom

Heroism, humility, and honor
Proudly acknowledges
Soldiers are the chosen ones
Called upon to handle
Such an enormous task
Carrying freedom of their country
Upon their courageous shoulders
Exemplifying true patriotism
Hearts of warriors

THE STAR-SPANGLED BANNER NATIONAL ANTHEM OF THE UNITED STATES

O say can you see
By the dawn's early light
What so proudly we hailed
At the twilight's last gleaming

Whose broad stripes and bright stars
Through the perilous fight
O'er the ramparts we watched
Were so gallantly streaming

And the rockets red glare
The bombs bursting in air
Gave proof through the night
That our flag was still there

O say does that star spangled banner
Yet wave
O'er the land of the free
And the home of the brave

REMEMBER TO SAY "THANK YOU"

*To All Those Who Serve, Have Served, OR Remembering
THOSE THAT HAVE died Serving And Their Families*

Their Sacrifice Exemplifies

HEROISM, HUMILITY, AND HONOR

—T.E. BROOKS

www.ingramcontent.com/pod-product-compliance
Lightning Source LLC
Chambersburg PA
CBHW021227020426
42331CB00003B/498